OUT WEST

A Guide to the Hidden Joys of the West Country

For Neil, Tommy and Danny for making these trips so much fun.

Published by
Pocket Mountains Ltd
The Old Church, Moffat, DG10 9HB
www.pocketmountains.com

ISBN: 978-1-907025-570

Printed in Poland

CONTENTS

ACKNOWLEDGEMENTS

Thanks to the owners, curators and custodians who run these remarkable attractions, often as a labour of love.

Thanks, too, to the readers and enthusiasts who have enjoyed earlier books in the series, and encouraged me to write this one.

INTRODUCTION

Way Out West is the third book in the bestselling *Nothing To See Here* series of travel guides. Unlike its predecessors, it happened almost by accident when a simple trip to North Cornwall – never designed to eke out the brilliant and the bizarre – unearthed a collection of unexpected treasures of such wealth and scope that a third volume became inevitable.

Sometimes wonderful things find you, and stumbling across places like the Hawker's Hut, Barometer World and the Boscastle Museum of Witchcraft proved that this intriguing part of the country could easily fill a book with its unusual and sometimes well-hidden attractions.

Further expeditions followed and the result is this collection that celebrates the less-than-ordinary destinations in the counties of Devon, Dorset and Somerset, as well as in Cornwall.

It's a particularly beautiful part of the world, full of enchanting scenery, fascinating history and buckets of charm. Travellers should note that the narrow roads and relaxed pace of life can mean it takes a while to get anywhere around these parts, so take your time to savour the joys of the West Country.

A LA RONDE

A la Ronde is the ultimate in English eccentricity. A specially-commissioned 16-sided house overlooking the Exe Estuary, it is remarkable outside and in. It was built in the 1790s for cousins Mary and Jane Parminter – remarkable women, who travelled widely and collected objects and ideas along the way. No ordinary home could do them justice, so they built an extraordinary one.

The squat hexadecagonal building looks more like a giant biscuit tin than a house. It might appear impractical, but when it was built, the south of England was under threat of invasion from France. The distinctive diamond-shaped windows made it harder to break in, and the doors that slide seamlessly into the walls to link each room not only save space, but allow the inhabitants to run a full circuit of the house if they need to escape in a hurry.

The architecture and interior fittings are a delight in their own small way. The house's unique shape creates plentiful nooks and crannies – all well used of course – with libraries shaped like a

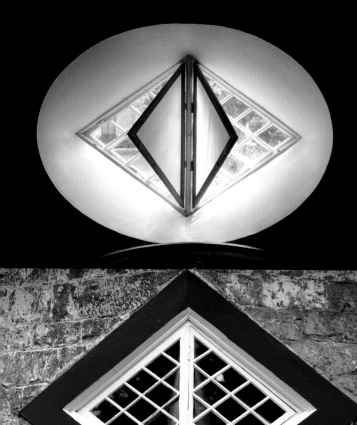

wedge of cheese, and shelves of nick-nacks stacked into odd corners.

Each room is filled with treasures from other worlds and other times. Paintings, prints and silhouettes adorn every wall; here an invitation to William IV's coronation in 1831, there a chair from Lord Nelson's ship. The Parminters kept themselves busy making delicate models from everyday materials and creating intricate papercuts with mind-bogglingly tiny scissors – these are also on display.

You'll find shells everywhere, from the basement kitchen to the roof. The circular Shell Gallery that fills the top of the house is said to be the most extensive of its kind, containing nearly 25,000 individually applied shells. Up here, they line every surface, supplemented by sticks, stones, feathers and anything else that helped to create a more intricate scene. The stairway to the gallery is a

miniature Gothic extravagance in its own right. The Shell Gallery is currently closed for restoration but you can view it from the octagonal hall that forms the centre of A la Ronde. The meticulously painted chevrons on the wall give it an undersea feel – just another small detail that makes A la Ronde seem like another world.

Now in the care of the National Trust, the Parminters' grand designs are being carefully looked after to amaze and inspire future visitors.

ACCESS AND OPENING TIMES

A la Ronde is on Summer Lane, Exmouth, South Devon, EX8 5BD and has a gift shop and tearoom. It is open daily from February to October. There is an entry charge for non-National Trust members.
www.nationaltrust.org.uk/a-la-ronde

10

THE ADMIRAL BENBOW

The Admiral Benbow on Penzance's historic Chapel Street is a real treasure trove. The model sniper lying on the roof tells the eagle-eyed passer-by that this is no normal pub. Inside it's a land-based temple of sea-going fun, with nautical memorabilia crammed into every available space.

Trading as a pub since the 18th century, the Admiral Benbow made waves in the 1950s when then owner Roland Morris brought his love of the sea back onto dry land. An accomplished deep-sea diver, his exploratory dives to historic wrecks yielded booty that now decorates the interior.

As you enter through the wooden doors covered with carvings of Neptune, it takes a moment to adjust your eyes to the dark interior. Model ships, salvage and maritime paraphernalia cling onto every surface like barnacles. Glass weights, nets and lifebelts mingle with the traditional pub ornaments of tankards, Toby jugs and horse brasses. Visit the bar and get into the spirit with a bottle of rum or a flagon of ale.

This is only a taste of what is yet to

come. The real glory is at the back of the ground floor, in the Great Cabin. This magnificent themed room is a recreation of a ship's cabin made from intricate carved wooden panels rescued from a Man o'War/privateer. There's a steering wheel in the middle of one table. You can almost feel it rocking as you eat your fish and chips.

Upstairs the Wreck Bar and the Lady Hamilton Bar are no less understated, with half-naked figureheads looming out of the darkness and a bar that looks like it's been decorated with the contents of a pirate ship's lost property box.

The discovery of tunnels running under the building in 2008 cemented the

Admiral Benbow's place in Penzance's maritime history. The Benbow Brandy Men would bring barrels of contraband up through the tunnels from the harbour to avoid detection. These days the clientele is more salubrious and it's the perfect place to drink in some atmosphere.

ACCESS AND OPENING TIMES

The Admiral Benbow can be found at 46 Chapel Street, Penzance, Cornwall TR18 4AF, and is open daily.

BABBACOMBE MODEL VILLAGE

Babbacombe Model Village (population: 13,000) is the largest model village in Britain, growing from a small collection when it opened in 1963 to hundreds of buildings sprawling over a scenic four-acre site near Torquay.

The village started out as an idyllic slice of country life – 'model' in more ways than one. Farms, cottages and country houses were surrounded by beautiful greenery. Today, these bucolic scenes still exist, but they are mixed with more familiar scenes from modern life. A family watches TV, teenagers play on a Playstation and mum sits at a laptop with a bottle of wine to hand.

There are noisy nightclubs, bustling train stations (with running trains!), factories, football matches, heliports and hospitals. The landscape has become more diverse over the years, with a new town centre featuring a towering Shard, a West Country fishing village, a castle with a fire-breathing dragon and a miniature Paignton Zoo. There is even a model model village, complete with working miniature railway. See if you can spot it!

Observe the villagers go about their daily business, picking up sweets from Annie Seeds, or booking a holiday with travel agent, Andy Waywego. While it is mostly an idealised representation of

HEALTHYWAY
HEALTH FARM
PROPRIETOR JIM. NASTICK

THE
CAVERN

WOMBLEY STADIUM

GROUND FULL · GROUND FULL · GROUND FULL · GROUND FULL · GROUND FULL · STAND B

modern life, watch out for the little misfortunes – a streaker disrupting the match at Wombley Stadium, a fire breaking out in a thatched cottage (convincingly made from coconut matting) and, in suburbia, an unhappy meeting between a garage door and a brand new car.

A dedicated team works tirelessly to keep the village spick and span. Trees and hedges are constantly clipped to keep the illusion of scale and the houses, much like real houses, need to be regularly fixed and repainted. Exhibitions highlight the amazing work of the model makers, with an *Eastenders* set and film scenes recreated in miniature.

Don't be fooled into thinking this is a small affair – there is so much to see that it takes at least two hours to get round. In summer, enjoy the evening opening when the village is illuminated by more than 14,000 lightbulbs.

ACCESS AND OPENING TIMES
Babbacombe Model Village is on Hampton Avenue, Babbacombe, Torquay, Devon TQ1 3LA and is open all year round. www.model-village.co.uk

THE BAKELITE MUSEUM

The Bakelite Museum in Williton is a modern treasure. There is something fantastically joyful about its single-minded devotion to the versatile substance that has been part of modern life for more than a century.

Developed by Leo Baekeland in 1907, Bakelite was the first synthetic plastic. Inflammable and resilient, it could be cheaply produced and easily moulded and coloured. It quickly became ubiquitous in modern homes, making everything from toys to teeth.

The Bakelite Museum is the finest collection of its kind anywhere in the world. Owner Patrick Cook has been

sniffing out Bakelite items for over 40 years and his collection is unrivalled, with everything from vacuum cleaners to a Bakelite coffin.

The stately brown radio sets that Bakelite is famous for are well represented here, but the museum goes way beyond that. There are clocks, radiators, hairdryers, adding machines and telephones. The small items like egg cups, napkin rings and a staggering array of cruet sets make this feel like the museum of the midcentury home. Everything is bright and resilient, and the colourful retro style has never really gone out of fashion, making Bakelite

items highly collectable today.

Bakelite's various ancestors and relatives are on show too, from early plastics like Bois Durci and Vulcanite to Shellac and the fantastically named Bandalasta and Linga Longa.

Considering the size and value of the collection, the museum is remarkably relaxed. If there's no-one on the door, leave the entry fee in the honesty box. The owner, who makes the wonderful 'pod' caravans on show outside, may float by, but he doesn't intrude. Very few of the exhibits are behind glass which adds to the loveliness as the feel and smell of the material is so evocative of times past. There is little explanation and few captions or signposting – there's no need as the exhibits speak volumes. Bakelite is beautiful, versatile and omnipresent and the world would be a duller place without it.

ACCESS AND OPENING TIMES
The museum is located at Orchard Mill, Williton, Somerset TA4 4NS and is open from 1 March to the end of October (and by appointment out of season). www.bakelitemuseum.net

BARBARA HEPWORTH MUSEUM AND SCULPTURE GARDEN

St Ives is a bustling Cornish town, loved by visitors who come to enjoy its generous beaches and rugged scenery. It is also a haven for artists who have flocked here for decades to find inspiration. During high season it can be hard to find a quiet spot, but keep climbing through the town to find the serenity of the Barbara Hepworth Museum and Sculpture Garden.

Barbara Hepworth is St Ives' most famous artistic alumnus, living and working here for more than 30 years until her death in 1975. She is most famous for making large abstract sculptures from wood, stone and bronze. The organic forms that somehow manage to simultaneously contrast with and complement their surroundings are internationally renowned, making Hepworth one of the 20th century's most successful female artists.

Born in Wakefield in 1903, Hepworth studied at Leeds School of Art where the trademark holes in her sculptures were said to influence classmate Henry Moore.

40

Please
do not touch the
works in this room

She first came to St Ives in 1939 with her husband, the artist Ben Nicholson, and young family. By 1949 she was internationally successful and needed space to work. A friend pointed her to Trewyn Studio, which was up for sale, and a beautiful partnership was born. This airy studio with an adjoining garden gave Hepworth the opportunity to work closely with the landscape that inspired her.

Today, the studio feels like it has been recently vacated. Blocks of stone sit waiting to be carved, cats nap, and cacti soak up the sun. Hepworth worked here for 25 years, changing her main materials from wood and stone to bronze. The garden that she designed with friend and composer Priaulx Rainier gave her space to design larger works and choose how to display them to their best advantage.

The studio is now in the care of the Tate Gallery and the permanent exhibition provides an inspiring introduction to Barbara Hepworth and her work. The chance to see inside the eye of a unique artist with such striking work in a beautiful location is a rare privilege.

ACCESS AND OPENING TIMES
The museum and garden are located at Barnoon Hill, St Ives, Cornwall TR26 1AD, within walking distance of St Ives town centre. They are open all year. www.tate.org

BAROMETER WORLD

Barometer World in Merton, Devon is primarily a business that sells, makes and repairs barometers. It is also home to the world's finest (and only) barometer museum.

Inside the Quicksilver Barn, with its clever entrance shaped like a weather house, there are barometers of all shapes and sizes. The informative exhibition, open by appointment only, tells the story of weather forecasting through the ages from lightning bottles and storm glasses to more modern aneroid and mercury barometers.

Although the subject could be quite dry, it is so much more interesting than you might expect. It quickly takes you back to a time before weather forecasts where knowing what the weather was about to do could be a matter of life or death.

As captain of Charles Darwin's ship *HMS Beagle*, pioneering meteorologist Robert FitzRoy certainly understood the importance of the weather. Now seen as the father of modern forecasting, he made daily weather predictions, coining the term 'forecast' in the process, before going on to establish what became the Met Office and create systems for sailors

and fishermen to receive accurate weather information. FitzRoy Barometers named after him can still be seen in coastal resorts today.

At the more fanciful end of the scale is a working replica of Professor George Merryweather's Tempest Prognosticator, first exhibited at the Great Exhibition in 1851. This ornate gold contraption is powered by leeches who ring an alarm bell to warn of a storm approaching. It is very accurate by all accounts, and the centre keeps one leech on permanent forecasting duty.

Natural forms of forecasting are a reminder of how much weather is a part of our life. Whether it's pine cones, red skies at night or flowers like the scarlet pimpernel (once called the Poor Man's Weather-Glass), speculating on the weather is a popular pastime. And it's not just a British preoccupation, as the museum's outstanding collection of weather houses from Germany shows.

Today we're more likely to tap an app than a barometer, so their wonder may not be clear to everyone, but the unflinching dedication of owner and barometer aficionado Philip Collins makes the science of weather forecasting really come alive.

ACCESS AND OPENING TIMES
Barometer World can be found at Quicksilver Barn, Merton, Okehampton, Devon EX20 3DS and is open by appointment only.
www.barometerworld.co.uk

BATH POSTAL MUSEUM

Bath Postal Museum celebrates the history of the postal service and Bath's vital place in it. For more than 25 years this small museum has carefully packaged the development of this vital service into an experience that is bags of fun. Don't miss its collection!

The museum traces the history of sending and receiving mail from its earliest days, from writing letters and stamping and posting them to the people and services that make sure they get to the right place at the right time.

A replica Victorian post office with quills and brown paper packages tied up with string sends visitors back to another era. There are unexpectedly beautiful things to see here. The collection of antique embroidered postcards is a joy to behold. A cross-written letter, where the text runs horizontally and vertically, was an extreme way of saving money when postage was charged on each sheet of paper. And the collection of crash and wreck mail, salvaged from air

Blotters were very important and stopped ink being smudged. They came in various shapes, or you could use a book of blotting paper.

In the Victorian age the Post Office asked people to put letter slots like this in their front doors to help deliver the mail more quickly.

Patriotic and uplifting postcards....Propaganda was being used long before the outbreak of World War 1, the use of posters and postcards were pioneered during the war

crashes and shipwrecks, is fascinating and poignant.

Bath's famous figures who made their mark on the postal world are suitably commemorated. In the 1720s, Ralph Allen, Postmaster of Bath, ran the South West's Cross and Bye Posts which allowed mail to be sent between provincial towns rather than going through London. In the 1780s, John Palmer saw an opportunity to use horse and chaise to transport mail. He talked the Royal Mail into trying a mail coach from Bath to London. It was so successful that it quickly became a permanent service.

Of course, no postal museum would be complete without stamps. The earliest known use of the famous Penny Black stamp happened here in 1840,

when Bath postmaster Thomas Musgrave sneaked one into the post a few days early. Popular philatelists such as Freddie Mercury, Franklin D Roosevelt and Maria Sharapova are also featured, and visitors are encouraged to have a go at designing their own.

ACCESS AND OPENING TIMES

Bath Postal Museum can be found at 27 Northgate Street, Bath BA1 1AJ and is open (with limited hours) all year round. www.bathpostalmuseum.co.uk

THE BILL DOUGLAS CINEMA MUSEUM

The Bill Douglas Cinema Museum is tucked away on the University of Exeter's leafy campus. It was founded when Scottish film-maker Bill Douglas and his lifelong friend Peter Jewell bequeathed their collection of early cinema artefacts and film memorabilia to the university with the instruction to create a museum that would help children to understand cinema.

The result is a world-class collection that goes beyond the history of just cinema. Douglas had a fascination with the development of moving pictures, and the museum showcases his collection of early forms of optical entertainment. There are shadow puppets, optical illusions, magic lanterns, panoramas and dioramas. Early advances in moving pictures can be experienced through zooescopes, mutoscopes and praxinoscopes with modern replicas available for hands-on entertainment.

The history of cinema is traced from the early days of silent movies right through to modern blockbusters. An emphasis on the cinema-going experience makes the collection familiar to everyone. The small,

evocative pieces of ephemera from playbills and tickets to Jaws paperbacks and Star Wars soap conjure up the excitement of being a film fan so realistically that you can almost smell the popcorn.

Objects from Bill Douglas' career are also on display. He was best known for *My Childhood*, *My Ain Folk* and *My Way Home* – a trilogy of films that told the story of his early life in Newcraighall near Edinburgh. Douglas' love for early cinema shines through in his own films, like the magic lanternist who tells the story in *Comrades*, a cinematic epic about the Tolpuddle Martyrs. The picture that develops is a man who

loved films in all their various forms.

Its loving dedication to all kinds of cinema, from silent films to sci-fi, *Carry On* to Kurosawa, means there's something for everyone. Only 1000 of the collection's 75,000 items are on display. It is also accessible as a research collection. This small but perfectly curated museum captures the magic of cinema for all ages and tastes.

ACCESS AND OPENING TIMES

The Bill Douglas Cinema Museum is open 7 days a week and is free to visit. University of Exeter, The Old Library Prince of Wales Road, Exeter EX4 4SB. www.bdcmuseum.org.uk

THE BLUE POOL

As the name suggests, the Blue Pool in Furzewood, near Wareham is a blue pool. Not any old blue, but a bright turquoise which makes nature look like a technicolour photograph. It is a beautiful and unexpected sight as it comes into view through the trees.

The pool's unusual colour comes from its former life as a clay pit. The clay particles suspended in the water refract the light in different ways, changing the water colour from grey to green to turquoise.

A small museum beside the café digs up the history of the area. The clay found here, known as Purbeck Ball Clay, is a rare and precious substance. Its white colour, fine grain and elasticity make it ideal for producing ceramics.

The demand for clay pipes in the 16th and 17th centuries fired up the industry, which continues to dominate the area today. In the 18th century, ceramics king Josiah Wedgwood proclaimed Purbeck Ball Clay to be the best in the world and ordered 1400 tons of the stuff. The high quality of the clay enabled him to manufacture thinner-walled ceramics and more refined products like his iconic blue and white Queen's Ware.

The Blue Pool was dug in 1845 and produced clay for the next 70 years or so. When it was left to flood it became a natural resource of a different kind and visitors have been enjoying this colourful spot ever since.

Set in 25 acres of heath and woodland, the pool is a centrepiece for a network of peaceful paths. Now a designated Site of Special Scientific Interest, it is home to a variety of unusual plant and animal species. Look out for Dartford Warblers, Sand Lizards, Marsh Gentians and Sika deer.

Four-legged inhabitants of a different kind also delight visitors in the Wareham Bears exhibition. This is a collection of more than 200 teddy bears carefully arranged into everyday scenes of shopkeeping, sports and socialising. It is furry entertaining!

ACCESS AND OPENING TIMES

The Blue Pool is located south of Wareham in Dorset, signposted from the Stoborough roundabout off the A351, and is open from 1 March to the end of November (the café is open from April to October).
www.bluepooltearooms.co.uk

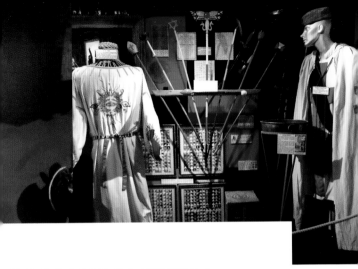

BOSCASTLE MUSEUM OF WITCHCRAFT

The idea of a witchcraft museum probably conjures up all kinds of ghoulish mental pictures, but the Boscastle Museum of Witchcraft is a thoroughly enchanting place.

Now more than 50 years old, it was established by Cecil Williamson, a neopagan witch and authority on witchcraft in the Isle of Man. It moved a few times, each time attracting hostility and threats until it came to rest in Cornwall where people are at home with piskies and otherworldly creatures.

The first thing that the museum gets across is that witchcraft goes far beyond the classic image of an old crone in a black pointy hat. The boundaries between witchcraft, superstition, folklore and religion are blurred. What instantly becomes clear is that most people have a little bit of witchcraft in their lives. Fortune telling and divination is common in different forms around the world, whether it's Tarot cards, crystal balls or tealeaves. Horseshoes, corn dollies, black cats, shamrocks and wishing wells are all seen as lucky, something you put your faith and hopes in that can't be grasped or seen.

So practices considered 'weird' maybe aren't so strange after all, especially when presented alongside more accepted religious beliefs. The attitudes to witchcraft and folklore are cast into sharp relief, and the persecution of believers is well-documented. The

37

shackles and scold's bridles used to persecute witches are also here, highlighting society's attitudes to unconventional beliefs.

There is a chance to see inside a witch's house. Joan Wytte died in Bodmin Jail in 1813 and her cottage is recreated here. Plants used for spells fill racks like a high-class herbalist, and intriguing items of witches' paraphernalia are on show, including spirit houses and hexing bottles. Witches or 'cunning folk' were there to help with everyday problems plaguing people's psyches. Irksome people could be banished with a Get Lost Box containing a representation of whatever you want to get rid of, to be left at a crossroads. Information on pagans, druids and wicca show that these beliefs live on, still on the fringes of society.

The ritual and sometimes darker side of magic is explored with some fascinating exhibits from the practices of satanism and Freemasonry. Some exhibits may alarm more sensitive visitors, but generally it is a spellbinding collection, arranged in a thought-provoking way.

ACCESS AND OPENING TIMES

The museum is located by the harbour in Boscastle, Cornwall PL35 0HD and is open every day from 1 April to the end of October. museumofwitchcraftandmagic.co.uk

BOSCOMBE PIER

Piers are remarkable things. Remnants of a former era when British seaside resorts were more thriving places, they stick their necks out against the tide in more ways than one. And they are all special in different ways. It may not be the longest, shortest or oldest, but Boscombe Pier, near Bournemouth in Dorset, has come to be known as Britain's coolest.

In contrast to the delicate wrought-iron and ornate detail of Britain's Victorian piers, Boscombe Pier is a modern streamlined affair. The audacious entrance building, with its cantilevered roof shaped like the wings of a jet, introduces a stylish pier where a minimalist windbreak casts an angular shadow along its length.

Like many of its peers (sorry) Boscombe Pier has also been through some hard times. Originally built in 1888, it had no head until 1926. It was partly demolished for security reasons during the Second World War and lay in a sorry state until the 1950s when the consensus was that Boscombe needed a lift. The pier was redesigned in the Modernist style by borough architect, John Burton. The pier neck was rebuilt in reinforced and pre-stressed concrete (so this one shouldn't burn down) and

the Mermaid Theatre at the head was opened in 1962 with the ultimate in modern entertainment – a roller rink.

By the 1990s the pier's future looked bleak again. Seaside resorts went out of fashion and the pier closed, only to bob back into fashion a decade later. Grade II listing cemented the pier's status as a British icon, and thoroughly modern couple Wayne and Gerardine Hemingway were brought in to rejuvenate the Boscombe seafront, turning tumbledown beach huts into desirable beach 'pods'. The successful regeneration and addition of Europe's first artificial surf reef saw it crowned Pier of the Year by the National Piers Society in 2010. Since then Boscombe has become a go-to destination for sun, sea and surfing in style.

ACCESS AND OPENING TIMES

Boscombe Pier is located on Sea Road, Boscombe, Dorset BH5 1BN and is open every day from 9am.

BRIDGWATER BRICK AND TILE MUSEUM

Bridgwater Brick and Tile Museum celebrates the humble housebrick and commemorates an industry that made Bridgwater famous around the world.

In the 19th century, the distinctive conical chimneys of bottle kilns became a familiar sight on the Bridgwater skyline. The clay deposits of the River Parrett provided abundant raw materials and at its height more than 18 brickworks along the river employed half the male population of the town. Bridgwater bricks became famous all over the world, building houses from New York to New Zealand.

The industry thrived until new production methods and modern materials laid the foundations for its decline in the early 20th century. Bridgwater's brickmakers closed one by one, until only Barham Brothers at East Quay remained. It fired its last brick in 1965 and was largely demolished in the 1970s. Thankfully, its distinctive bottle kiln was saved as the last of its kind. Now a Scheduled Ancient Monument, it has been enclosed in a building designed to look like a plain tile-drying shed.

Inside, photographs and catalogues from the Barham Brothers archive and other local collections show the surprising varieties of bricks, pantiles and decorations produced here, including the distinctive dragon-shaped tiles that adorn the roof of the museum.

Get your hard-hat on for a look inside the kiln, and watch a video about how bricks are made. Racks of tiles and chimney pots make it feel like the last shift has just ended. Displays introduce the vocabulary of brick-making from pugging to extrusion, and tools are there for eager hands to play with.

This free museum run by enthusiastic volunteers tells its remarkable story in an understated way, constructing a vivid shrine to the humble brick and the industry that formed the fabric of the local area. Spend some time here and you will soon see bricks in a different light.

ACCESS AND OPENING TIMES

The museum is located at East Quay, Bridgwater TA6 4DB and is open on Tuesdays and Thursdays.
www.swheritage.org.uk

BUCKFAST ABBEY

Buckfast Abbey is an idyllic spot in a peaceful part of Devon. The stately abbey sits in beautiful grounds where the only sound is birdsong and bees buzzing around the well-kept gardens. There is nothing unusual about this scene, unless you know the name of Buckfast from an altogether rowdier association – the popularity of its home-brewed tonic wine amongst teenage drinkers.

Made to a traditional French recipe, 'Buckie' as it's more commonly known was first bottled in the 1890s and sold as a medicine before becoming a tonic wine in the 1920s. To this day, no-one quite understands how it became so popular with the nation's underage and street drinkers, particularly in the area of central Scotland bordered by the towns of Airdrie, Coatbridge and Cumbernauld known as the Buckfast Triangle.

At 15% ABV (Alcohol By Volume) and with more caffeine than Red Bull, it certainly packs a punch. The green glass of smashed Buckie bottles is a familiar sight the morning after the night before, and crime statistics link it to an average of three crimes a day, giving rise to colourful nicknames like Wreck the Hoose Juice and Commotion Lotion.

Anti-social behaviour is not something that the Abbey's monks are in the habit of, and the drink's distributors have fought to distance themselves from its lively reputation. Anyone expecting a Buckie factory shop or line of ironic souvenirs will be sorely disappointed. Instead, the focus here is on quiet contemplation. Blue-robed monks glide through the grounds, and silence reigns inside the grand abbey which was completed in 1938. A modern chapel added in 1966, specifically for contemplation and silent prayer, is a particularly peaceful spot.

Today, the Abbey's focus is on education with a conference centre onsite and a special department dedicated to beekeeping. The shop does sell its famous brew alongside Chimay, Chambord and other drinks made by religious communities, as well as honey produced here by the specially-bred Buckfast Bee.

ACCESS AND OPENING TIMES
Buckfast Abbey is half a mile from the A38, midway between Exeter and Plymouth and entrance is free.
www.buckfast.org.uk

BURGH ISLAND

Burgh Island is a very stylish destination, tucked away at the end of a long and winding road in a scenic part of South Devon. A part-time island, it is connected at low tide to Bigbury-on-Sea, a popular coastal spot for surfers and walkers.

There isn't a lot to it, but what's there is rather special. The Burgh Island Hotel, a streamlined Art Deco affair, shines bright white against the landscape.

This stunning building has had many famous guests, including the Beatles and Winston Churchill. It was a favourite haunt of Agatha Christie, who used it as a setting for some of her stories. Noel Coward came for three days and stayed for three weeks. It's that sort of place.

Those who do book are promised an authentic 1920s experience with full dinner dress every night and strictly no TVs in the room. Access to the hotel and grounds is strictly for guests only, and the island's one pub, the 13th century Pilchard Inn, operates a similarly exclusive door policy for guests and regulars only.

Visiting riff raff are still welcome to walk on public parts of the island. There is a clearly signposted path to a viewpoint with a huer's (fisherman's) hut. Clambering around this windy spot is a good way to blow away the cobwebs.

When the tide is out you can walk to

the island across the sandy beach but, even when the tide is not so obliging, visitors can still get across by hitching a lift on the island's specially-designed sea tractor. This tractor has an extendible platform which can raise itself 7 feet off the ground and still traverse the soft sand. It may not be the most stylish way to travel, but it's certainly different.

The long road to Burgh Island is worth travelling to see this coastal gem.

ACCESS AND OPENING TIMES
Car parking at Bigbury-on-Sea.
www.burghisland.com

BURNHAM-ON-SEA PIER

Poor Burnham-on-Sea Pier, so short that it's barely there at all. Where most piers stretch out into the distance majestically, Burnham's offering only just gets its feet in the water. At 274m it is officially Britain's shortest, almost 2000m shorter than the world's longest pier in Southend.

This dinky little thing is Burnham's second pier. The first was built in 1858 further along the shore, and connected with the local railway line to bring Victorian pleasureseekers to the

paddlesteamers to Wales. This route didn't last long, but Burnham-on-Sea kept its place as a popular seaside resort for a while longer.

Built between 1911 and 1914, the new pier was remarkable for its time. The first concrete structure of its kind in Europe, rumour has it that the pier was built as an experiment. Engineers came from miles around to admire it, while locals were more sceptical, expecting it to be swept into the sea by the first tide. The pavilion that covers it shares some design features with the grander buildings of Isambard Kingdom Brunel, a master builder around these parts.

What it lacks in length it makes up for in enthusiasm, with flags flying from all corners of the roof, amusements packed inside and ample opportunities for chips, ice-cream and other seaside staples. The waters of the Bristol Channel, with the second highest tidal range in the world, make this a place of extremes. The curvaceous concrete sea wall, built in 1988, protects the town against storm surges, and at low tide the mudflats stretch out for more than 2km, officially a wetland of national importance. While on the beach, look out for Burnham's distinctive low lighthouse, small but perfectly formed – just like its pier.

ACCESS AND OPENING TIMES
Burnham-on-Sea Pier Pavilion can be found on the Esplanade, Burnham-On-Sea, Somerset, TA8 1BG.
www.burnham-on-sea.com

CHALK FIGURES

Geoglyphs – drawings and carvings on the earth – are found worldwide, some dating back thousands of years. Sometimes their meaning is clear and in other cases, like the Nazca Lines in Peru, they remain a great mystery. In the UK, the most common type is the chalk figure, mainly found in the south of England where the distinctive white soil and rolling hills make them visible for miles around.

White horses are the most popular, with more than 50 in the UK. One that stands out is the Osmington White Horse in Dorset. Sculpted into the hills north of Weymouth in 1808, this horse is unique in having a rider. The figure in question is King George III who enjoyed visiting Weymouth on holidays.

Some 17 miles away, the Cerne Abbas Giant is one of only two human chalk figures in the UK – the other is the Long Man of Wilmington in Suffolk. At almost 60m tall, you can't miss him, and once seen he is never forgotten. It's not every day that you see an angry naked man waving a club at you from a hillside.

Remarkably, his nakedness and unmissable gigantic erect penis is tolerated, nay celebrated, in a nation famously prudish about such things. No-one quite knows how he got there or what he represents, but theories range from it being an ancient fertility symbol to a representation of the god Hercules or a satirical cartoon.

We may never know for sure, as attempts to pin down his origins have been unsuccessful. The earliest recorded mention of him was in 1694 and since then he has led an interesting life, regularly visited by couples hoping to conceive, and periodically repainted to keep him spick and span.

He was camouflaged in the Second World War and more recently adorned with a giant pair of trousers, an enormous purple condom, an Olympic Torch, a grass moustache and a red nose for Comic Relief. He also gained a temporary friend when a naked Homer Simpson brandishing a doughnut was drawn alongside him to promote *The Simpsons Movie* in 2007.

ACCESS AND OPENING TIMES

Osmington White Horse – there is a car park and viewing area off the A353 between Osmington and Weymouth. The Cerne Abbas Giant – now managed by the National Trust, there is a car park and viewing area off the A352 or a short walk from Cerne Abbas village.

CHARLESTOWN SHIPWRECK AND HERITAGE CENTRE

The Charlestown Shipwreck and Heritage Centre is not your average maritime museum. It is almost the opposite, in fact. Where lovingly restored ships usually stand proud alongside tales of derring-do at sea, here you'll find wrecks and ruins, disasters and emergencies. It's like a gritty behind-the-scenes drama full of peril and tragedy.

The largest private collection of its kind stretches underground, winding through the tunnels once used to carry clay to the waiting boats. Charlestown was the only outlet for the St Austell area, shipping clay, china and copper to foreign climes. The grand harbour is now Grade II listed, still operational and historically intact. It has been used as a film set for the likes of *Poldark*, *Doctor Who* and Tim Burton's *Alice in Wonderland*.

Inside the museum, Charlestown Road tells how the town developed, with scenes showing local life through the ages. Like many Cornish towns, the

residents live by the sea in more ways than one. A display of ornate rope knots show the artistic side of nautical life with everything from a standing Turk's Head to a Monkey's Fist.

There are estimated to be a quarter of a million shipwrecks in British waters, and the blackspots all feature here from Goodwin Sands, a series of sandbanks in the English Channel, also known as 'the ship swallower', to Scapa Flow in Orkney, overflowing with wrecked German warships. There are items from famous shipwrecks like the *Mary Rose*, *Torrey Canyon* and of course, the *Titanic*.

With wrecks come divers, and the museum's history of diving is fascinating. It shows how far diving equipment has come from wooden diving barrels to aqualungs. The atmospheric displays really get across the challenges that divers face. Finding treasure must be a great reward, and there's plenty of that here from crockery to coins and cannonballs from more than 150 salvaged shipwrecks.

The remarkable thing about this museum is seeing beyond the romantic vision of striped shirts and fishing boats to the gritty warts-and-all reality of rocky coasts, rough seas and the heroism of those who work on them.

ACCESS AND OPENING TIMES

The Shipwreck and Heritage Centre can be found on Quay Road, Charlestown, St Austell, Cornwall PL25 3NJ, and is open from April to October.
www.shipwreckcharlestown.com

CLOVELLY

Clovelly is one of England's few private villages, owned by the same family for generations. It is also one of the most picturesque, with a steep cobbled street lined with colourful cottages leading down to a sheltered harbour.

After paying the entrance fee at the top of the hill, a steep descent awaits all visitors. The main street is too narrow and steep for road vehicles so the only access is for pedestrians and the occasional donkey, and it's a push for them too. The sledges that you see lining the street are not a gimmick, that is genuinely how people transport their shopping.

Every building on the main street is listed, so there are plenty of excuses to stop and take photos. Colourful hanging baskets spill out from the doorways, and gargoyles leer out from unexpected places. If you want to stop for longer, the Kingsley Museum is worth a visit. Novelist Charles Kingsley moved here, aged 11, while his father was rector. The museum explains how his idyllic childhood led him back to Clovelly time and time again. He even used it as the setting for his novel *Westward Ho!* after which the Devon town was named. While you're there, the Fisherman's Cottage near the museum shows village life during the 1930s.

Further down the hill, look out for Obergammergau Cottage with its decorative woodcarvings, brought all the way from Germany in 1910 by Clovelly's owner Christine Hamlyn. After that, enjoy the view from the Look Out before descending to the harbour for some fresh seafood or a stiff drink at the Red Lion.

Clovelly is well-served by shops and cafés, so if you need fortification on the way back up, treat yourself to a delicious Devon cream tea (cream first, then jam). For those who find the walk too steep, there is a Land Rover taxi service from the harbour, transporting weary visitors back to the top of the hill.

ACCESS AND OPENING TIMES

Clovelly is just off the A39, 10 miles west of Bideford. Open all year, there is an entry fee to the village.
www.clovelly.co.uk

DEVON ROAD SIGNS

There are so many things to see in Devon that the weird world of road signage is easy to overlook. However, eagle-eyed road users may notice that signs are a bit different round Devon way. Get away from the main roads (perfectly conventional as these things go) to find the standard colours of green for major routes and black and white for main A- and B-roads replaced by a colourful gallimaufry of wayfinding.

Devon's distinctive road signs are the regulation size and shape, with the same familiar Transport typeface. But they are blue and brown, or black and white with no borders and strange hollow chevrons. Once you notice that something is amiss, it's an enjoyable car game to look for the others and wonder what on earth they mean. Even the top code crackers may struggle, though, as the signage is rather erratically applied.

Legend has it that the key to their meaning can still be found in a Dartmoor car park, but apart from that, there are (as far as we're aware) few if any public explanations of the signs.

Some internet research yields an explanation from the SABRE website. The system was introduced around Dartmoor in the 1980s to guide visitors around the often narrow local roads. Blue signs point to non-primary A- and

B-roads, suitable for medium-sized vehicles. Brown is one level smaller – suitable for cars and small vehicles. The black and white signs are reserved for very narrow roads where you can expect to enjoy the Devon pastime of hedge-surfing. The lowest class of roads are signified by traditional wooden finger posts.

In some of the larger towns, there is another set of symbols – colourful stars and triangles that suggest to the untrained eye that the circus is coming to town. Sadly their function is more mundane, helping to guide heavy goods vehicles to industrial estates and other exciting locations.

You've got to admire the pluck of this quirky system – an attempt to make road signs more useful for visitors and the car journey more colourful in the process.

DINGLES FAIRGROUND HERITAGE CENTRE

Dingles Fairground Heritage Centre is a real treat – a permanent fairground indoors, so it's fun come rain or shine. In a somewhat out of the way location in Lifton, Devon, it is well worth the trip with enough to occupy visitors for hours.

Dingles is more than just your average fairground. It is home to the National Fairground Collection, where historic fairground equipment is carefully preserved and maintained for new generations.

The collection may lack the terrifying rollercoasters and vertiginous rides that theme parks are known for, but it is no less entertaining. Here you'll find classic rides such as carousels (known here as 'gallopers'), switchbacks and scenic railways with enticing names like The Supersonic Skid and The Moonrocket.

Informative displays put each ride into its historic context, bringing them to life before they even have any passengers. The development of the machinery is engagingly explained, along with social changes (such as the improvement of transport) that enabled

fairground rides to develop and their popularity to grow.

As well as being highly entertaining, the rides are a work of art. The unsung artists who created the remarkable signs and banners that add so much atmosphere are given their due here, with dedicated displays of fairground art and biographies of the most notable players. The scenes they painted were often signs of the times, showing everything from the rise of the British Empire and space exploration to the swinging '60s and Madonna.

As well as the rides, other favourites include the Hall of Mirrors, Coconut Shy, Bingo stall and a whole array of vintage slot machines. A beautifully-restored travellers' caravan opens a door to a way of life so separate from the visitors who came to the fair for some thrills.

The importance of the Dingles collection has been cemented by support from the Victoria and Albert Museum for its artistic interest and the Science Museum in preserving the historic rides. Whether you visit as a museum or a working fun fair it's a grand day out.

ACCESS AND OPENING TIMES

Dingles Fairground Heritage Centre can be found at Milford, Lifton, Devon PL16 0AT. It is one mile from the A30 in West Devon, 7 miles east of Launceston, and is open 7 days a week from early March to the end of October. www.fairground-heritage.org.uk

DORCHESTER TEDDY BEAR MUSEUM

The Teddy Bear Museum in Dorchester shares a building with the Terracotta Warriors Museum, just round the corner from the Dinosaur Museum. Rather softer in nature, the museum is a shrine to the UK's favourite cuddly toy.

Visitors are greeted by Edward Bear and his family of human-size teddies who inhabit the museum. They go about their daily business – knitting, listening to the gramophone, having a quiet snooze. There are bears of all shapes and sizes wherever you turn, some worth thousands of pounds and others of little monetary value, but all very precious to their dedicated owner.

The museum traces the birth of teddy bears back to 1902 when US president Theodore 'Teddy' Roosevelt famously refused to shoot a bear tied to a tree because it was unsportsmanlike. A cartoon in the *Washington Post* lampooned the event and the name Teddy Bear was born.

Meanwhile in Germany, the Steiff Company of Giengen made its first toy bears for the 1903 Leipzig Fair. An

A rare pair of 1960's boy (blue) and girl (pink) Schuco bears. German.

American spotted them and ordered 3000 for export. Steiff bears, with their trademark button in the ear, are still the most valuable today, and the museum has some prime examples on display along with more modern collectables from Charlie Bear and Merrythought.

Although the majority of the collection features traditional teddy bears, other bears are not forgotten. Look out for SuperTed, Fozzie, Rupert and Yogi among others. As you browse, the warm voices of human teddy bears Stephen Fry and Alan Bennett read stories from *Winnie the Pooh* and *Paddington*. A display of fancy-dress bears is a pun-lover's paradise, featuring the Follies Beargere, Albeart Einstein and even Libearace.

The museum is a real honeypot for teddy bear enthusiasts and is accessible for non-experts too. Cuddly toys feature in most childhoods and the Teddy Bear Museum manages to gently recreate the feeling of a warm hug through joyful displays of its soft, gentle inhabitants.

ACCESS AND OPENING TIMES

The Teddy Bear Museum is located at Eastgate, on the corner of High East Street and Salisbury Street, Dorchester, Dorset DT1 1JU and is open all year. www.teddybearmuseum.co.uk

EGYPTIAN HOUSE

The ornate and colourful façade of the Egyptian House comes as something of a surprise, popping out of the classical buildings of Penzance's Chapel Street. Like its countrymate, the Sphinx, it retains an air of mystery. Records show that it was designed for John Lanvin in the 1830s as a museum and geological repository, but beyond that few details are known.

What is clear is that it's an absolute delight, a multicoloured wedding cake crashlanded into a small town high street. Words cannot adequately describe it, but picture if you will, a three-storey building. On the ground floor, two lotus-bud columns flank a recessed doorway topped by a flamboyant sundisk traditionally added to ward off evil. The window frames are

in the trapezoid 'pylon' shape that is a trademark of the Egyptian style and are filled with geometrically-patterned windows.

On the first floor, feast your eyes on a pair of caryatids with fabulous head-dresses, and keep looking skywards to find the distinctly un-Egyptian royal coat of arms. In case that wasn't quite enough, a giant eagle rampant tops it off.

It is likely that its design was based on England's first Egyptian-style building, Robinson's Egyptian Hall, which was built in London's Piccadilly in 1812. This encapsulated the vogue for all things Egyptian and started a trend for Egyptian-style buildings that continued for decades.

Surviving Egyptian buildings are few and far between (London's Egyptian Hall was demolished in 1905) and this one is lucky to survive. After falling into disrepair it was bought in 1968 by the Landmark Trust, a charity that preserves historical buildings at risk. Now carefully restored, the relatively normal regency interiors have been converted into three holiday apartments for rent.

ACCESS AND OPENING TIMES

The Egyptian House is on Chapel Street, Penzance, Cornwall TR18 4AJ. To book the holiday apartments, go to www.landmarktrust.org.uk

HAWKER'S HUT

Hawker's Hut in Morwenstow is currently the National Trust's smallest property. What it lacks in size it makes up for in character. Nestled into a North Cornwall cliff face looking out to the Atlantic Ocean, it is a fragile-looking thing, cobbled together from driftwood and goodwill. It looks like a stiff breeze could blow it over, but tenacious like its owner, it has survived for more than 150 years in this sheltered spot.

To appreciate the hut, you first need to enter the weird world of the Reverend Robert Stephen Hawker (1803-1875). Rector of Morwenstow Church, he was a renowned eccentric who reportedly always wore brightly-coloured clothes and once excommunicated his cat for mousing on Sundays. The first clue to his singular vision is in the chimneys of the rectory that he built beside the church. Look carefully and you will see they are built in the form of tiny steeples, as a tribute to the places he lived before moving to Morwenstow.

The Church of St John the Baptist and St Morwenna, where the Reverend was vicar from 1834 to 1874, reveals more about his colourful life. He was a compassionate man who began the tradition of Harvest festivals here in 1843 when he thanked God for a bountiful

harvest. He was also notably kind to shipwrecked sailors, of which there were many on this rocky coast, burying them with dignity. The figurehead of the ship *The Caledonia* in the churchyard marks the grave of its crew who were lost in 1842.

Allegedly some of the wood from these wrecks was turned into the Hawker's Hut. To find it, follow the path from the church across the fields towards the coast. At the coast turn left onto the coastal path and continue until you see a National Trust marker. Go down the steps and there it is. Inside is a simple wooden seat and a stable door that allows you to close the bottom half against the wind and still enjoy the sea view.

This is where the Reverend spent his spare time smoking opium, writing poetry and entertaining his famous friends such as Alfred Lord Tennyson and Charles Kingsley. The timbers are covered with carved initials of visitors old and new. It feels like time has stood still here and a moment gazing at the sea from Hawker's Hut will bring out the poet in you.

ACCESS AND OPENING TIMES
To get to Morwenstow, turn off the A39 at Stratton near Bude and head north to Stibb. Pass Stow Barton, go down through woodland and pass the GCHQ station before turning left for the village (Morwenstow, Cornwall EX23 9SR). www.nationaltrust.org.uk

HELSTON FOLK MUSEUM

Helston Folk Museum is a wunderkammer of local life in this Cornish town most famous for its Furry Dance.

Housed in what was the town's local market and drill hall, the surprisingly extensive collection covers every aspect of local life on the Lizard Peninsula, from day-to-day business to annual traditions. Local museums can be hit or miss, but it's all hits here. Each object seems to be interesting in its own right, or have a story behind it. Behold the miniature dice made from a lion's tooth, some hairballs found in the carcass of a bullock and the bell used by Mr Harry Clifton of Meneage

Steet to summon customers for ice-cream in 1922.

There is everything from scrumpy jars and butter pats to Serpentine stone. Bygone traditions are on display from a coopers' workshop to a doctor's surgery. And the small objects of domestic life speak volumes, like ear trumpets, candle snuffers and moustache cups. The area's more famous residents are represented too. Five links of chain from Marconi's masts at Mullion commemorate his work on wireless communication.

Helston's main claim to fame is its annual Flora Day, held every year on

8 May (unless it falls on a Sunday or Monday). The town celebrates the Feast of the Apparition of St Michael the Archangel, the patron saint of Helston, with a series of dances – furry means feast or holy day but the dance is more commonly known as a floral dance. The tune emanating from the museum's majestic Furry Clock will be instantly recognisable to those old enough to remember Terry Wogan's unexpected hit from 1978.

The other part of Flora Day is the Hal-an-Tow, a processional dance where a Helstonian dressed as St Michael fights a dragon while the townsfolk wave sycamore branches. For this reason, a huge paper dragon hangs over the main hall. Luckily he looks like a friendly type.

This mix of peculiar old customs, fascinating local exhibits and a glimpse of days gone by make Helston Folk Museum a fantastic day out.

ACCESS AND OPENING TIMES

Helston Museum is located on Market Place, Helston, Cornwall TR13 8TH. It is free to visit and open all year (except on Flora Day). www.helstonmuseum.co.uk

J.V. GEACH, M.B.E.
(1881-1975)
Mr. Geach was a local carpenter
and undertaker, reputed to have
made his own coffin and sat in it
regularly to read "The West Briton".
He was a well-known Methodist
Preacher, and Chairman of
Kerrier Rural District Council
from 1953-54.

THE HOUSE OF MARBLES

As its name suggests, the House of Marbles in Bovey Tracey is devoted to the humble sphere that has been a well-loved plaything for hundreds of years. Whether you enjoy a game of marbles, play solitaire with them, or just roll them around in your hand they are beautifully simple objects – easy to overlook but utterly perfect in their own way.

This glass and marble museum gives the tiny toy its moment of glory. Beautifully arranged display cases trace the history of marbles through the ages, showing off the many different styles available, from the simple and familiar to the complex and collectable.

Before glass marbles were invented, pebbles or nuts did the job. Early marbles were made from clay or earthenware before the glass marble was introduced in the 1860s. It would be easy to think that marbles are always the same, but they are a diverse bunch with a rich vocabulary. Visit the museum to see rainbows, oilies, onion skins, Benningtons and clears, alongside the classic 'leaf' pattern.

The museum also has a fine display of those medical marbles, glass eyes, and a large collection of classic board games,

MAN-MADE STONE MARBLES

To our knowledge there is only one factory left making these in southern Sweden. This marble-making technique uses a machine that resembles a cement mixer. The machine is filled with a slurry comprising plaster cement, talc and pigment. Tiny rape seeds are thrown into the mixer and roll around inside. As they become more, they begin to pick up a coating of the mixture, gradually increasing in size and becoming round. Several hours later during the process coloured dyes are added to give the marbles their required colour.

In 1999 a second factory opened in Holbæk Sweden.

such as solitaire and bagatelle. Their simple pleasures will take many a visitor back to childhood.

The craft of marble-making is revealed through a display of vintage machinery, with glass-blowing demonstrations at regular intervals. There is a constant reminder of marbles' tactile beauty as they pitter-patter through complex marbles runs, including the UK's largest designed by Alexander Schmid.

The House of Marbles also has a pottery museum full of Bovey Tracey pottery. Weymss Ware, with its characterful cats, was produced here from the 1930s to the late 1950s after moving from Kirkcaldy in Scotland during the Great Depression. The distinctive muffle kilns are preserved as Statutory Ancient Monuments. There is also an excellent shop, with a marble pick and mix. Something for the whole family to enjoy.

ACCESS AND OPENING TIMES

The House of Marbles can be found at The Old Pottery, Bovey Tracey, Devon TQ13 9DS and is open to visitors all year. www.houseofmarbles.com

THE ISLAND, PENDINAS

The Island, in St Ives, is not really an island at all. Technically it is a peninsula, joined to the town by a narrow strip of land. The small chapel-topped hill, jammed between Porthgwidden and Porthmeor beaches, provides a quiet space away from the coastal crowds, and an impressive viewpoint for this stunning part of the Cornish coast.

Originally knows as Pendinas, meaning fortified headland, the Island has had many adventures in its day. In prehistoric times it really was an island, cut off from the mainland at high tide. In the Middle Ages, it housed a promontory fort and, in the 1860s, a granite battery was built in case Napoleon came to call.

The charming one-roomed church that tops the island off is dedicated to St Nicholas, the patron saint of sailors. A chapel for centuries, it became a lookout for tax officers in the 19th century, later becoming a war store.

In 1904 it was deemed obsolete and partially demolished until the mayor intervened and it was saved. The contrite War Office handed it over to the town, and the building was resurrected. It opened fully as a chapel again on 6 December, St Nicholas's Day, 1971.

The Island is also home to Lamp Rock, a guiding light for fishermen and now home to a National Coastwatch station. Over the years this stretch of coast has had a string of exotic visitors from migrating seabirds such as skuas and shearwaters, to artists and writers seeking inspiration. The author Daphne du Maurier stayed locally in Downalong. Perhaps St Ives' notoriously vicious seagulls were an inspiration for her novel *The Birds*.

This quiet spot, a short detour from St Ives' bustling main drag, feels like a holiday within a holiday. The little island feels like it's built from layers and layers of history, and the stiff breezes and whirling seabirds are sure to blow the cobwebs away on the climb towards the gentle calm of the little chapel.

ACCESS AND OPENING TIMES

St Ives is on the north Cornish coast, west of Camborne and 20 minutes from the A30.

ISLE OF PORTLAND

The Isle of Portland deserves a mention here as one of England's hotspots of weirdness. It's hard to put your finger on what exactly is so strange about it, but for a relatively small area it is a thrill ride of unexpected encounters, surprising views and peculiar architecture.

To start at the very beginning, the isle is reached via a barrier beach, linking it to the skinny wonder that is Chesil Beach and the Jurassic Coast beyond. When you reach the island, the road climbs past grand buildings made from

Portland Stone. You can't escape that here – it is the home of this amazing weatherproof stone used in famous buildings worldwide, from St Paul's Cathedral to the UN Headquarters in New York. Wherever you go, lumps of rock and big diggers seem to follow, giving the sense of a place that is always under construction.

Near the top of the island, Verne Citadel suddenly appears. A grand Victorian fort built to protect the south coast from marauders, it was a Category

C men's prison from 1949 to 2014 and is now an Immigration Removal Centre. Beside it, the high angle batteries, built in 1892, are the best-preserved examples of their kind. The concrete is sturdy and the gun emplacements seem freshly vacated. A view into the working quarry below shows the stone that Portland is famous for.

On the southern tip of the island, known as Portland Bill, its distinctive red-and-white striped lighthouse stands proudly looking out to sea. Now a visitor centre, a guide will take you to the top and tell stories of this tumultuous coast. One lighthouse is not enough for a rocky coast like this, so there are three. One is now home to Portland Bird Observatory and the other is a private residence, open to visitors who want to stay awhile in this remarkable place.

Before heading back to the mainland, don't miss Portland Sculpture Park. Formerly Tout Quarry, a short walk through the rusting tramlines and derricks reveals open-air sculptures by Antony Gormley and other prize-winning artists.

If you feel creative you can have a go yourself, with enormous blocks of Portland stone ready to be transformed. Just don't mention rabbits, they are considered to be bad luck here and are never mentioned by name.

ACCESS AND OPENING TIMES
The Isle of Portland is 5 miles south of Weymouth in Dorset.

JAMAICA INN

Jamaica Inn sits stolidly on Bodmin Moor, looming out of the mist like something from a horror film. Somehow, it manages to sit beside the busy A30 road and still feel like it's in the middle of nowhere. Bodmin Moor is an odd place at the best of times, and this historic hostelry appears to have absorbed centuries of weirdness until Cornwall's history is embedded in its solid oak beams.

Built in 1750, it was a travellers' rest, mainly for smugglers and 'wreckers' who lured ships to the rocky Cornish coast to steal their cargo, then headed to the towns with their loot. Another visitor, the novelist Daphne du Maurier, stayed here in 1930 and found it so inspirational she turned her experiences into the novel *Jamaica Inn*, published in 1936.

Still a working pub, the building has atmosphere seeping out of every crevice. The bar is dark and snug, with a roaring fire and period memorabilia adorning every available surface. Intrepid guests who want to stay longer can hire one of the hotel rooms and take part in a ghost hunt or murder mystery weekend.

The inn also houses the intriguing Museum of Smuggling, with one of the largest collections of its kind. It paints an atmospheric picture of these dangerous

JAMAICA
INN

days, with wanted posters, dioramas, and an intriguing display of concealed contraband.

Daphne du Maurier also has a permanent place here. Her desk, with Sheraton typewriter and dish of Fox's Glacier Mints (her favourite, apparently) looks like it's recently been vacated, as the author nips out for an inspirational cigarette.

Sadly, the inn no longer houses Mr Potter's Museum of Curiosities, a remarkable taxidermy collection created by Mr Walter Potter in the 1850s, displaying small stuffed animals in extravagantly detailed everyday poses such as going to school and playing tennis.

It is well worth a visit to drink up the atmosphere or something stronger if you prefer.

ACCESS AND OPENING TIMES

The Jamaica Inn is found at Bolventor off the A30 between Launceston and Bodmin, Cornwall PL15 7TS. www.jamaicainn.co.uk

LANDMARK THEATRE

The Landmark Theatre in Ilfracombe is not your usual theatre, thanks to its unusual double conical design. At first glance it looks like a couple of windmills that have lost their sails or a pair of off-duty cooling towers. Locals found a comparison from popular culture, and nicknamed the building 'Madonna's bra' – a fitting reference for those who remember Ms Ciccone's eye-watering undergarments.

Tim Ronalds Architects who completed the building in 1997 approached the brief creatively. The Victorian Theatre that stood on this spot since the 1920s was in dire need of repair. Most theatres are only designed to be attractive from the front, but because of its exposed location, in the centre of town with Capstone Hill overlooking it, they designed the Landmark to look good from all sides.

The ground floor, containing the foyer, nestles into the cliff while the towers rise above it on either side. A grass roof connects the building to the coastal path, anchoring it to the cliffside. The sea air can be cruel, and any replacement building needed to

be hardy. The two cones are 22.5m high and made from more than 300,000 Belgian china-clay bricks.

One tower contains the main house, a round theatre with seating for 480. The other contains the Pavilion – a multi-purpose space flooded with natural light. Viewpoints look out to sea and Capstone Hill. The austere exterior is softened inside by lines from local poet Ted Hughes.

Fans of the unusual may also enjoy the Clapping Space near the theatre, an acoustic oddity where a single clap echoes loudly off the surrounding landscape. Other attractions in Ilfracombe include hand-carved Victorian tunnels leading to sheltered beaches and a tidal bathing pool, and Damien Hirst's controversial 20m-high statue *Verity*, which watches over the seafront, rarely leaving viewers indifferent.

ACCESS AND OPENING TIMES
The Landmark Theatre is on Wilder Road, Ilfracombe, Devon EX34 9BZ.

LAND'S END

Robert Louis Stevenson said that it is better to travel hopefully than to arrive, and many feel that is true of Land's End. Mainland Britain's most south-westerly point (the most southern is Lizard Head a few miles away) is one end of Britain's most famous long-distance route and the start (or finish) point for the 'End to Enders' who traverse 874 miles (1349 km) for charity or pleasure by foot, bike, horse and even skateboard. A marked Start and Finish line at the entrance to the village regularly fills up with friends and relatives waiting to welcome or wave off their intrepid loved ones.

The best way to enjoy Land's End is to avoid the tourist village and explore everything surrounding it. The traditional whitewashed buildings look striking against the Cornish skies and deep blue sea, and the area is home to many species of plants and animals.

The walk from the village to the First and Last House is one of the real highlights as dedicated travellers go the extra mile to the tip of the headland and back again. This regular pulse of visitors has the feel of a beating heart.

Look out for landmarks; Dr Johnson's Head and Dr Syntax's Head on the craggy coast. Seals, basking sharks and

dolphins can be seen in the water, and nesting seabirds like puffins and Cornish choughs make the rocky cliffs their home. An RSPB information centre is open from spring to autumn, and a number of walks can be enjoyed around the local area.

Don't miss the model village situated randomly beside the play park – a small but perfectly-formed collection of traditional houses from the local area. There's also the famous signpost of course, if you don't mind paying the fee for a souvenir photo.

ACCESS AND OPENING TIMES
Land's End is at the end of the A30, 8 miles from Penzance. Parking charges. www.landsend-landmark.co.uk

MINACK OPEN AIR THEATRE

The Minack Theatre's open-air setting on a Cornish cliff 4 miles from Land's End sees it regularly (and rightly!) applauded as one of the world's most spectacular theatres.

This remarkable place is the brainchild of a remarkable woman. In 1929, some locals performed *A Midsummer Night's Dream* on a meadow near the Minack. When they were looking for somewhere to stage *The Tempest*, Rowena Cade, who lived in Minack House, had the idea of using the cliffs below as a dramatic setting. Most people would have dismissed this idea straight away, but Rowena Cade was not your average person. She built the theatre out of the rock, literally with her own hands, and worked through two winters with the help of her gardener to get the stage ready. When the Minack's first performance opened in 1932, the stage was a grass terrace and the lights ran off car batteries. It was still a roaring success.

For the next 50 years until her death in 1983, Rowena Cade kept building the theatre by hand. The granite cliffs provide the dramatic backdrop, with the seats, steps and fittings all moulded from cement mixed with local sand. If you take the steep path up to the

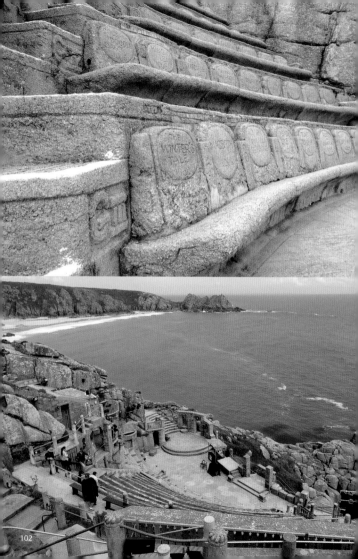

theatre from Porthcurno beach you get a small taste of what a difficult labour this must have been. Picture that journey while carrying rocks and bags of cement in fair weather and foul. It's a miracle that the theatre was built at all.

What is even more remarkable is that it has so many beautiful details. The motifs and patterns carved into the wet concrete and the hand-drawn names of plays on the back of the carefully-moulded seats bring the flair and tradition of the theatrical world to this rocky, exposed spot. You would never imagine concrete could have so much character, but the Minack successfully combines the grandeur of a Roman amphitheatre with the warmth of a community hall.

In the exhibition centre, actors and players talk of the unique challenges of playing there. There's the weather for one thing, plus seals and seagulls vying for the limelight and the sea air eating away at the equipment. Human chains are formed to get scenery and props in and out. This could be a headache anywhere else, but it's part of the privilege of performing here. The sub-tropical garden is as colourful and dramatic as the performances themselves.

ACCESS AND OPENING TIMES

The Minack Theatre is open from 1 March to the end of October and is located just south of Porthcurno, Cornwall TR19 6JU (follow the A30 almost all the way to Land's End before turning off at Trevescan and following the signs). www.minack.com

MONTACUTE TV AND TOY MUSEUM

The Montacute TV Toy and Radio Museum is a treasure trove of childhood treats. Crammed into a house and its outbuildings behind a cavernous shop and welcoming tearoom, the museum contains an outstanding collection of radio and TV memorabilia. More of a shrine than a museum, the exhibits are displayed with total reverence in an approachable way, all to worship the world of popular entertainment.

Worzel Gummidge, Aunt Sally and Mr Bean welcome visitors from behind a bank of vintage TV and radio sets. Proceed through the corridor of Western memorabilia with everything from dolls to annuals to snowstorms. Was there any series that didn't have a board game? Swashbucklers are interspersed with characters from *On The Buses*, while a life-size Rocky Balboa towers over the Flowerpot Men. Patrick McGoohan is not a free man here either, standing guard over vintage issues of the *TV Times*.

There are Wombles, Smurfs and the entire cast of the Magic Roundabout. Sci-fi gets a lot of shelf space with *Thunderbirds* and *Space 1999* leading to a corridor of Doctor Who characters (some quite terrifying) and an actual Tardis where the doctors mingle.

No depths of obscurity go unplumbed

– there are definitely more Worzel Gummidge toys than is strictly healthy, as well as Annie Sugden's wooden Aga from Emmerdale Farm. The Dan Dare radio set and *Emergency Ward 10* toy hospital show that merchandising is nothing new. Stills and theme tunes are here too, beside comics and annuals. Every last piece of memorabilia is lovingly displayed.

Well-loved TV characters can see out their twilight years here. Two Power Rangers seem a little lost among the novelty radio sets, like bouncers at a kids' party, but the Diddymen and the Krankies look like they're having a good

time and The Simpsons, Mork and Mindy and Juliet Bravo all come along for a ride.

The museum opened to the public in 1989, but its history goes back to the 1920s when local man Dennis Greenham ran a repair shop on the premises. He loved television and radio and his family have nurtured his fantastic collection for your viewing pleasure.

ACCESS AND OPENING TIMES
The museum is open from 1 April to the end of October and is located on South Street, Montacute, Somerset TA15 6XD. Montacute is 4 miles west of Yeovil. www.montacutemuseum.co.uk

THE NORMAN LOCKYER OBSERVATORY

Sir Joseph Norman Lockyer (1836-1920) was quite a guy. An eminent scientist and astronomer he is best known for discovering the element helium. He was passionate about improving science education and the observatory that he founded in London became the Science Museum. He was also Britain's first professor of astrophysics and a prolific author who founded the journal *Nature* and wrote about everything from physics to the rules of golf.

After his retirement in 1913, Lockyer established an observatory near his home in Salcombe Regis near Sidmouth in Devon. Originally known as the Hill Observatory, the site was renamed the Norman Lockyer Observatory after his death in 1920.

The observatory holds three historic telescopes. The Kensington Telescope

observatory has state-of-the-art facilities.

Its lofty location on a south-facing cliff provides perfect conditions for astronomical observation. The sky is relatively 'clean' in astronomy terms and its outlook over the sea means it is free of rising air currents that can affect optical images. This makes the observatory an ideal spot for amateur astrology, meteorology and radio.

Now owned by East Devon District Council, it is run by the Norman Lockyer Observatory Society who approach the study of astronomy with the same zeal and generosity as their founder. The centre celebrated its centenary with a new 20-inch reflector telescope and the opening of the new Lockyer Technology Centre by star and star enthusiast Dr Brian May. Links with the Universities of Exeter and Plymouth and the Open University bring in budding scientists, who can watch the skies for evidence of asteroids and meteors.

The site is open to members and to visitors on specially arranged open evenings.

from 1894 was used at the South Kensington Observatory to measure the temperature of stars, beginning the start of astrophysics research. The Lockyer telescope of 1863, which Sir Norman used to discover helium, kickstarted the science of solar physics, and the McClean telescope was donated by Sir Francis McClean to help found the observatory in 1912. Two more modern telescopes ensure the

ACCESS AND OPENING TIMES

The Observatory is located on Salcombe Hill Road, Sidmouth, Devon EX10 0NY and the dates and times of public openings can be found at www.normanlockyer.com

OVERBECK'S

The drive to Overbeck's up the long, steep road from Salcombe is like a metaphor for the man that gives the house its name. Otto Overbeck was always striving to reach new heights and he lives on in Overbeck's, the house bequeathed to the National Trust as a museum in his memory.

Born Otto Christoph Joseph Gerhardt Ludwig Overbeck to cosmopolitan Dutch/Italian-Prussian-French parents, he worked as a research chemist. In his professional life he almost invented Marmite and successfully brewed an innovative non-alcoholic beer, which sadly never made it to market.

Outside work he was an accomplished swimmer, experimental gardener,

linguist, artist, inventor and keen fisherman who caught the world's largest carp in 1902. He was also an avid collector, making Overbeck's a collection of museums under one roof. There's a maritime room, mini-museum of childhood, photography exhibition and natural history collection interspersed with the odd possessions of Overbeck and his family.

The star exhibit is the polyphon, a rare mechanical music maker that plays oversize metal discs. Built in the 1890s, polyphons were quickly overtaken by more advanced player pianos and gramophones. Now only three of these are left and its intricate music fills the house regularly throughout the day.

After admiring the polyphon, don't miss the invention that made Overbeck his fortune. A firm believer in electrotherapy, his 'electrical rejuvenator' was designed to keep the owner young and beautiful by passing an electric current through their skin. This idea took off in the 1920s, earning enough to buy him the house as a retirement home. Sadly it was not enough to keep him alive to his projected age of 126, and he died in 1937 at the age of 77.

Outside the house, the spectacular gardens overlooking the Kingsbridge Estuary make a walk in these beautiful surroundings even more of a pleasure. Exotic and sub-tropical plants thrive in the warm Salcombe microclimate to make a striking Mediterranean-style garden in the heart of Devon.

Like the house itself, the garden is made up of odd collections and artefacts – there is a statue garden, banana garden, Secret Garden, Rock Garden and a Gazebo Garden, all full of colourful plants that you wouldn't expect to find in this quiet corner of England. Overbeck's is full of surprises – don't miss it.

ACCESS AND OPENING TIMES
Overbeck's is found at Sharpitor, Salcombe, Devon TQ8 8LW and reached by a narrow, winding country lane which is not suitable for large vehicles. The house is open from 13 February to the end of October and entry is free for National Trust members.
www.devonmuseums.net

PLYMOUTH HOE

Plymouth Hoe is a beautiful area of green space at the heart of Plymouth's historic seafront. Not to be confused with Westward Ho! which is a different thing entirely, this Hoe takes its name from the Anglo-Saxon word for a sloping ridge shaped like an inverted foot and heel. This picturesque hill has seen it all come and go over the years, leaving behind a collection of buildings that turn a scenic coastal stroll into an impromptu history lesson.

At the eastern end, the imposing Royal Citadel looms over the horizon, keeping the citizens of Plymouth in their place. Britain's most impressive 17th-century fortress, it is still in use today as home to the 29 Commando Royal Artillery.

Nearby, the red-and-white hoops of Smeaton's Tower are a cheering sight. This lighthouse was originally built on Eddystone rocks in 1759 and most of it was transported here in 1882. Restored to its original condition, visitors can climb 72 feet to the top to learn about its clever construction. The views from

the top make the trip worthwhile, particularly the bird's-eye view of Tinside Lido, a spectacular outdoor swimming pool opened in 1935 and built in the Art Deco style. Recently restored, it was voted one of the top 10 outdoor pools in Europe.

Along the coast, the three-storey Belvedere keeps watch over Plymouth Sound and Drake's Island. Further up the hill, graceful Victorian terraces enjoy the view. Their neighbour, the Sir Francis Drake Bowling Club, commemorates the

spot where he reportedly finished a game of bowls before leaving to fight the Spanish Armada in 1588.

These days, the Hoe is home to locals and visitors enjoying one of the many concerts and displays that make use of its spectacular landscape, or simply strolling through time.

ACCESS AND OPENING TIMES
Tinside Lido is open from May to September; Smeaton's Tower is open all year round. www.visitplymouth.co.uk

POLDHU RADIO STATION AND MARCONI'S HUT

Cornwall's Lizard peninsula is home to a pair of telecommunications hotspots where a man in a shed changed the world.

That man was Guglielmo Marconi. An Italian inventor and electrical engineer, he travelled to England at the age of 21 to find a better reception for his experiments with wireless broadcasting. His pioneering work on this quiet coast led to the wonderful world of radio and wi-fi that we depend on today.

A flat expanse of land on the cliff edge at Poldhu was where Marconi transmitted the first transatlantic wireless signal in 1901. A repetition of the Morse letter 'S' was received at Signal Hill in Newfoundland. The original buildings were demolished, but Wireless Field beside the new radio station still contains the footprint of the old station and the vast antennae. Nearby, a memorial to Marconi stands proudly looking out to sea.

A new visitor centre, opened exactly

100 years after he sent the first signal, tells the remarkable story of Marconi and his team, and provides a home for Poldhu Amateur Radio Club.

Near Lizard Point, accessible by a challenging coastal walk, Marconi's small wooden hut has been restored by the National Trust. Set up in 1901 as a research centre and monitoring station for Poldhu Point, it is the only surviving Marconi hut and has been restored to its original condition with a spark transmitter and coherer receiver that visitors can see close up. It is also a working radio station, home to future Marconis.

What was accomplished in these small huts led Marconi to a Nobel Prize for Physics in 1909 (shared with Karl Ferdinand Braun) for services to wireless telegraphy. Both of these places are fascinating to visit, to feel like you are stepping in Marconi's footsteps. The comparison with the development of submarine telegraphy at Porthcurno is also fascinating, and transmits the message that this quiet corner of Cornwall has been vital for modern telecommunications.

ACCESS AND OPENING TIMES

The Marconi Centre can be found at Poldhu, near Mullion, Cornwall TR12 7JB. Check marconi-centre-poldhu.org.uk for opening times. The Wireless Station is located 1 mile east along the coastal path from Lizard Point car park. Entry is free for National Trust members and opening times can be found at www.nationaltrust.org.uk

POLPERRO

In Cornwall, you will never go short of scenic fishing villages full of ice-cream shops and Cornish pasty emporiums. Polperro has all of this, with some added quirky attractions that make a longer stay worthwhile, all in a very compact space.

Firstly, like many harbour villages in the South West, cars are not allowed in the town centre. Instead, drivers are encouraged to park at Crumplehorn Farm, the large car park at the northern end of the village and either walk in or take the Polperro Tram. The tram is quite a sight. Not a tram at all, it is a milk float disguised as a miniature double-decker bus which will transport you to the village centre for a fee.

The narrow main street runs towards the harbour, forking across the River Pol that gives the village its name. The left fork is called The Warren for reasons that will become clear, and this network of tightly-packed houses is worth exploring. Look out for the famous Shell House, decorated with pictures and decorations made from seashells, including local landmark, Eddystone Lighthouse. The intriguing Heritage Museum of

Smuggling & Fishing paints a colourful picture of Polperro's history through the ages.

Back in the heart of the village, don't miss Polperro Model Village and Land of Legend. It is a quirky attraction that combines a small but perfectly formed model of Polperro (complete with shell house and model of the model village) with an interactive display combining the story of Cornwall's industrial past with its magical history.

On the other side of the river is the beach and harbour where fishing boats land their catches and pleasure boats

zip along the coast to Looe and Fowey. The whole place is full of interest, so it is small wonder that so many artists come here to try and capture its distinctive charm.

ACCESS AND OPENING TIMES

Polperro is 25 miles west of Plymouth and 6 miles west of Looe. There is no access for vehicles during the summer. www.polperro.org

PORTHCURNO TELEGRAPH MUSEUM

At first glance, there isn't much to separate Porthcurno from other Cornish coastal villages where a windy road leads down to a picturesque beach. Look closer – the thick cables poking out of the sand might give you a clue to what put it on the map. The sheltered bay made a perfect landing spot for the transatlantic undersea cables that revolutionised the way we communicate – by 1920, Porthcurno was the world's largest telegraph station, with 186,000 miles of cable converging on this unassuming spot.

Porthcurno Telegraph Museum uses the former telegraph station to tell this incredible story. For 100 years, telegraphs were sent all over the world from here, until the station closed in 1970. Enthusiastic guides, many of them former staff, talk engagingly about the birth of cable communications – a remarkable string of developments that meant a message could reach the other side of the world in minutes instead of weeks. In these days of email and instant messaging, it's easy to take these things for granted. Here, visitors can

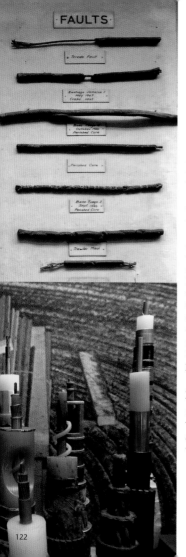

FAULTS

have a go at learning Morse code and marvel at the mind-bogglingly complex logistics of laying cables under the sea.

Telegraph's vital role in the war effort is engagingly explained, and no visit is complete without a visit to the wartime tunnels that run under the museum. These are virtually unchanged since the 1940s and the period equipment and wartime ephemera make the work of a telegraph operator come to life.

The museum is the largest and best developed of the area's many cable and wireless hotspots. Ironically, the development of wireless communication by Marconi, who also experimented in this part of the world, sealed the telegraph's fate as a means of communication. Its place in history can't be challenged though, and the pioneering developments are no less impressive today than they were 100 years ago.

ACCESS AND OPENING TIMES

The Telegraph Museum is located at Eastern House, Porthcurno, Cornwall TR19 6JX. The museum, café and shop are open from 1 April to end of October. www.telegraphmuseum.org

122

POUNDBURY

Poundbury, Prince Charles' ideal village near Dorchester, is a right royal oddity. Not an old town or a new town, it pokes its head round various architectural doors, never quite managing to come in.

Founded in 1993, Poundbury was conceived as an extension for the quaint Dorset town of Dorchester. The use of Duchy of Cornwall land gave HRH Prince Charles the chance to put his burgeoning architectural ideas into a new town with a difference. Architect and urban planner Leon Krier was engaged to realise the vision of

a town with character and heart, providing a mix of housing and priority for pedestrians.

Poundbury has grown in distinct stages, evolving as it goes. Its early phase was based on Dorset architecture with quaint cottages, gravelled pavements and twee street names such as Pendruffle Lane and Pummery Square, leading architectural critic Jonathan Meades to describe it as a 'Thomas Hardy theme-park for slow learners'. Later stages have spread their architectural wings into what can seem like pastiche – Regency-style

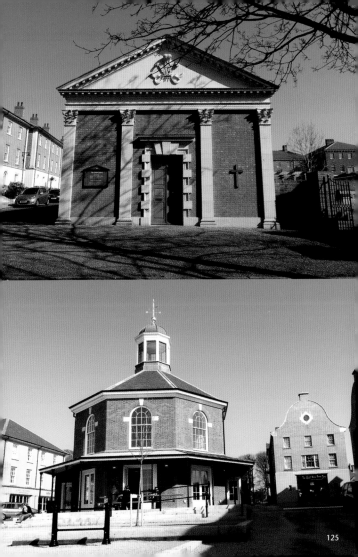

townhouses look onto the Butter Market where exclusive shops replace traditional market stalls. Most recently the outlandish Queen Mother Square, lined with Greco-Roman style creations such as the palatial Strathmore House, burst onto the scene like a giant wedding cake.

Carefully managed by a strict set of guidelines, Poundbury's trademark is a tightly-managed eclecticism where architectural styles are borrowed and appropriated into a new whole. One inspiration for this was Portmeirion, the remarkable Welsh village designed by Williams Clough-Ellis. Its mix of quirky Italianate buildings by the sea is delightful, except when it appears in nightmarish form in cult 1960s series *The Prisoner*. Somehow, Poundbury manages to ape the vibe of the latter,

where the too quiet streets, sparklingly clean buildings, hidden lanes and lack of signage give the whole place the unreal air of a giant model village or a dystopian film set.

It has its critics, but it has its fans too – residents like this quiet, carefully managed way of life. Although it's easy to scoff, it's not like anywhere else. On a sunny day it is truly beautiful and the overarching oddness makes any visit like a trip into another dimension. As proto-Poundburys pop up around the country it has a lasting legacy. Unoriginal and best.

ACCESS AND OPENING TIMES
Poundbury is located to the west of Dorchester off the A35.
www.princeofwales.gov.uk

THE RUSSELL-COTES ART GALLERY AND MUSEUM

The Russell-Cotes Art Gallery and Museum is a fascinating place. Perched on a cliff, a short walk from the town centre, it is Bournemouth's very own Taj Mahal.

Sir Merton Russell-Cotes was a colourful character: hotelier, Mayor of Bournemouth, keen traveller and art collector. His wife Annie liked to travel with him, and together they picked up all kinds of treasures from exotic journeys overseas. East Cliff House (as the building was originally known) was specially built as a present for Annie's 66th birthday in 1901, making it one of the last grand Victorian houses to be built in the UK.

Inside the main hall, light floods in through the stained glass roof illuminating the lavish decorations on almost every surface. It is a sumptuous affair, grand but gentle, with potted palms and even a small fish pond. The stained glass dome above the staircase shows the night sky, complete with owls and bats, and the frieze around the

balcony is a replica of the Elgin Marbles. It may sound slightly over the top, but the whole effect is wonderful. It is easy to forget that there's an art gallery still to come.

Many rooms are themed, often inspired by the couple's travels. Look out for the Mikado's Room, overlooking the Japanese Garden. Or the Moorish Alcove, inspired by the Alhambra in Granada. They were also keen patrons of the arts, and one room is dedicated to their friend, the actor Sir Henry Irving. The fittings are no less impressive, with an octagonal table once belonging to Napoleon Bonaparte and Queen Victoria's old sofa.

Four spacious galleries contain an outstanding collection of art and sculpture, particularly from the Pre-Raphaelite school. There are also temporary exhibitions and special events for all the family.

Bournemouth is lucky that the generosity of the Russell-Cotes' left this to the town. It opened to the public in 1919 and has been delighting townspeople and visitors ever since.

ACCESS AND OPENING TIMES
The Russell-Cotes Art Gallery and Museum is 2 minutes walk from Bournemouth Pier on the East Cliff Promenade, Bournemouth, BH1 3AA. It is open all year, but closed Mondays. russellcotes.com

SEATON TRAMWAY

Seaton Tramway is a way to travel in style and see a beautiful part of Devon at the same time. The 3-mile route links the Jurassic coast town of Seaton to historic Colyton. A fleet of 14 heritage trams shuttle along the banks of the Axe Estuary, giving passengers a bird's eye view of local wildlife.

The tramway was opened in 1971 by Claude Lane, a tram enthusiast whose scenic tramway in Eastbourne was being crowded out by cars. As luck would have it (or not, depending on how you look at it), Dr Beeching had swung his axe on the London & South Western Railway branchline to Seaton. The route existed; all it needed was a new lease of life.

The tramway's narrow 2ft 9in gauge made it a good retirement home for the petite trams of Bournemouth, Exeter and London Metropolitan Tramways. As the tramway grew in popularity so did the fleet, with new trams cleverly converted from larger models or built from scratch and painted in the livery of great British tramways. So if you see a green and cream 'Open Boat' Blackpool tram or a distinctive single-decker 'Toast-rack' car from the Manx Electric Railways, it is not lost but perfectly at home.

Once you've spotted the trams, look

out for the Axe Estuary's other attractions. The nature reserves of Seaton Marshes and Colyford Common are home to more than 50 varieties of bird and other animals. Wetland birds like egrets and herons nest on the lake, kingfishers dart along the river and crows and buzzards perch on the overheard wires. The local wildlife seems quite at home with their electric visitors as rabbits hop across the tracks, and badgers rudely burrow under them. Special birdwatching trips run regularly with expert guides. It's not called 'a bird hide on wheels' for nothing.

It's such a special day out that it's no wonder Seaton Tramway carries more than 100,000 passengers each year. And if you have a burning ambition to drive one, just book one of their special trips.

ACCESS AND OPENING TIMES
Seaton Tramway is on Harbour Road, Seaton, Devon EX12 2NQ. Check the timetable at www.tram.co.uk

THE SHALDON TO TEIGNMOUTH FERRY

Teignmouth-Shaldon Ferry, or the Shaldon-Teignmouth Ferry, depending on which side of the River Teign you're standing, claims to be England's oldest passenger ferry. Local records show a ferry crossing here as far back as 1296. Connecting two scenic Devon coastal towns, it is a valuable public transport link and an enjoyable jaunt in its own right.

The ferry itself is a jolly little thing, a small longship-style boat with a capacity of 35, although that must be a tight squeeze. There is no glamorous ferry terminal – look out for the sandwich board on the back beach near Teignmouth Lifeboat Station and the shelter along the beach from the Ferry Boat Inn at Shaldon.

The crossing takes roughly five minutes, weaving through the busy harbour full of boats, passing alongside sandy beaches with cheerily painted beach huts. Zipping across the River

Teign in this way saved a 14-mile round trip by road. Nowadays, a bridge makes this journey easier, but it isn't quite as much fun.

Teignbridge District Council operate the service, running two boats – No 4 (built in 1946) and No 5 (formerly the Kings Lynn Ferry, built around 1973). Their distinctive black and white decoration recalls the Napoleonic wars when fake gunports were often added to ships to make them look more imposing. The colourful bunting offsets this fearsomeness, however, so they are more like carnival floats than gunships.

ACCESS AND OPENING TIMES

Ferries run regularly (subject to the weather) every day apart from Christmas Day and New Year's Day. The nearby Teignmouth & Shaldon Museum on French Street, Teignmouth TQ14 8ST is also worth a visit for more local heritage and nautical history. www.teignmouthshaldonferry.co.uk

SHEPPY'S CIDER MUSEUM

Somerset is known for its cider, and the Sheppy family have been producing their own distinctive brand for more than 200 years. In that time, farming has changed dramatically and Sheppy's Cider Museum shows how rural life has changed through old photographs, obsolete machinery and a trip through Sheppy's own archives. It might sound dry, but it's actually rather sweet.

A short film shows the modern cider-making process, including the magical moment when apples are shaken off the trees with a gigantic mechanical arm and then hoovered up with what looks like a street sweeper. It's hard to believe that delicious cider comes from this shaky start, but the museum explains the whole process beautifully.

In 1894 there were 24,000 acres of orchards in Somerset producing bitter cider apples like the colourfully-named Crimson King, Slack-ma-Girdle, Harry Master's Jersey and Buttery Door. The great names continue in the old farming machinery – look out for the five-pronged eel spear, the potato riddle and the oat bruiser.

Cider always seems like an unpretentious drink but in the 17th century, it was more popular than wine. Sparkling cider was made by the champagne method and drunk from flutes. It was also looked on as a healthy drink, leading workers to carry cider in small wooden casks called firkins or castrels to be drunk with horn cups that they carried in their pocket. Special cider cups, some holding up to three pints, also feature in the traditional Wassail. Each January 5th this pagan ritual takes place to mark the winter solstice. In some places boys climb trees to offer cider-soaked toast to the birds as a mark of respect to the orchards.

More than 50 percent of Somerset's orchards have been lost since the 1950s, so it's more important than ever to preserve this heritage. Sheppy's Cider Museum is a great way to get a taste of Somerset cider-making. It's so interesting that it can even be enjoyed sober. If this makes you thirsty, there is a shop on site.

ACCESS AND OPENING TIMES

Sheppy's Cider Limited is located at Three Bridges Farm on the A30, just south of Bradford-on-Tone, between Taunton and Wellington in Somerset (TA4 1ER) and is open all year round. www.sheppyscider.com

EEL SPEAR
For catching Elvers out of rivers such as the Parrett.

THE SHOE MUSEUM

The Somerset town of Street is dominated by the footprint of brothers Cyrus and James Clark, who founded their famous shoe company here in 1825. It's only fitting that the Shoe Museum is shoehorned into their factory on the main street.

When you think about the vital role shoes play in everyday life, their history is relatively overlooked. The Shoe Museum puts that to rights, taking visitors on a walk through the history of footwear, from Roman sandals to stilettos and everything in between.

Carefully curated displays show shoes for the well-heeled. There are dainty pumps, ornate slippers and delicate baby shoes. On the other foot, there are clod-hopping clogs and ginormous jackboots. There are block heels, kitten heels, wedges, waffles and winklepickers.

There is also a great display of Clarks' foot-measuring machines – a rite of passage for many British children. Who doesn't remember having their little foot squashed into one of those? Their sturdy shoes have always come in a range of fittings, making them a reliable and popular make for growing feet.

The displays of Clarks' designs will be a trip down memory lane for visitors

The Reynolds children (great-grandchildren of James Clark)   about 1913

CHILD

1910 Infant's Ankle Strap. or "Tackie". Upper and sole of brown goat. Tackies were machine stitched inside out, turned, put on a last and left

1910 Infants Ankle Strap.

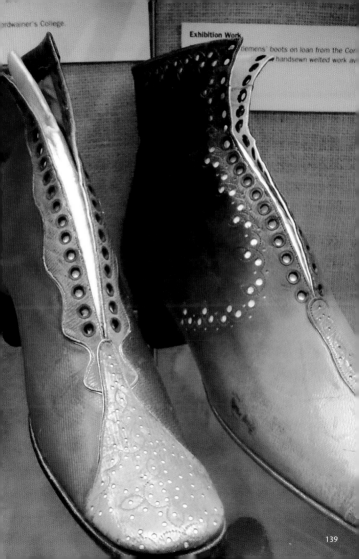

Exhibition Work

emens' boots on loan from the Cor
handsewn welted work av

1936 'Le Touquet'

1937 'Sark Sandal'

who remember striding out in a new pair of Commandoes. Men's shoes are heavily outnumbered in the exhibition, but the few that appear make their presence felt, whether it is 'Steve', the imposing platform boot, or 'Gavin' the towering crepe. The range of fashions is quite staggering, and a thoroughly entertaining thing to look at.

Clarks' symbol, Glastonbury Tor, anchors them to this beautiful part of the world. A family of Quakers, they treated their staff well and created amenities in the village that are still used today. A history of the company steps back in time to explain how 'outworkers' were

based at home before factories became mechanised. Some houses in Street were specially built with backshops – special rooms accessible by ladder for working at home.

On the whole, the Shoe Museum is a thoroughly surprising place to visit. Its sure-footed telling of shoe-making history is quite a feat.

ACCESS AND OPENING TIMES

The Shoe Museum can be found on the High Street, Street, Somerset BA16 0EQ, not far from the Clarks Outlet Village. It is open all year. www.the-shoe-museum.org

1941 Casual Shoe

the fashion success

Clarks

Lady's Evening Bar Shoe.
patent, multi-coloured brocade underlay. 2½" louis
urnshoe. Made and lent by Bally, Switzerland.

1923 Lady's Court
White calf, brown s
wn. Made and len

141

THE TOLPUDDLE MARTYRS MUSEUM

The Tolpuddle Martyrs Museum tells the story of six remarkable men who fought for what they believed in and changed society in the process. Their principled stand and subsequent struggle for justice is widely regarded as the birth of the modern labour movement, making the small Dorset town of Tolpuddle a focus for social justice campaigners to this day.

The location of the museum gives visitors a clue to the town's stirring story. A row of six cottages built by the TUC includes a library that now houses the small but informative museum. The story of the martyrs is told through a series of illustrated banners – a medium much loved by the labour movement.

It is quite a story. In 1832, the Industrial Revolution was transforming the agricultural industry, and farm labourers found it harder to find work. Wages fell to six shillings a week, not enough to sustain a family. Facing destitution, six men from Tolpuddle met secretly and swore an oath to form the Friendly Society of Agricultural

143

Labourers. They pledged not to work for less than 10 shillings a week.

Hearing of this alliance, local squire and landowner James Frampton was outraged. At the time, unions were legal, but secret oaths were not and the arcane Mutiny Act of 1797 was used to arrest the Tolpuddle men. The establishment was against them, and they didn't stand a chance of a fair trial. They were found guilty but instead of the standard punishment of seven days imprisonment, they were sentenced to seven years transportation to Australia.

This injustice garnered great support, galvanising the early trade union movement who campaigned for their release. The men were finally pardoned in 1837 and allowed to come home. James Hammett was the only one to return to the village.

Their story has never been forgotten, and Tolpuddle has been a focal point for activists ever since. A Memorial Arch outside the church was erected in 1912. In 1934, the centenary of their sentence, the TUC built six cottages and erected a thatched memorial shelter beside the Martyr's Tree. The annual Tolpuddle Martyrs' Festival is organised by the TUC on the third Sunday in July and regularly attracts big-name politicians and campaigners who treat the journey to Tolpuddle as a spiritual pilgrimage.

ACCESS AND OPENING TIMES

The village of Tolpuddle is off the A35 between Dorchester and Poole in Dorset (DT2 7EH). The museum is free to visit. For opening times visit; www.tolpuddlemartyrs.org.uk

TREMENHEERE SCULPTURE GARDENS

Tremenheere Sculpture Gardens occupy a beautiful spot overlooking the coast near Penzance. In a sheltered valley with views across the bay to St Michael's Mount, subtropical plants co-exist with modern sculptures. It is hard to say which one is more dramatic.

The impressive landscaping is designed to work in natural harmony with the 20-acre site. In what feels like around the world in 80 plants, there are dark and shady woods, arid cactus gardens, calming ponds, fecund bogs and open lawns. The garden's microclimate allows subtropical plants from the Mediterranean and beyond to flourish. In case a beautiful garden wasn't enough, it's also an al fresco gallery of modern art.

Some of the artworks blend in so well

with their surroundings that they are tricky to spot. A line of long grass by renowned landscape artist Richard Long could easily be mistaken for shoddy mowing. And Kishio Suga's pieces use bamboo and logs to make statements about modern society. On the other hand, James Turrell's Tewlwolow Kernow is most definitely man-made. This chamber set into the hillside has an elliptical hole for a roof. Relax inside and watch the Cornish sky roll past. Similarly, Billy Wynter's camera obscura is an unexpected way to see this beautiful part of the world from a different angle.

The growing art collection is the brainchild of owner Dr Neil Armstrong, who has transformed this overgrown spot into a garden that has something worth seeing at any time of year. Stroll round Tremenheere and you will feel like you have travelled further than a corner of Cornwall.

ACCESS AND OPENING TIMES

Tremenheere Sculpture Garden is located 2 miles east of Penzance near the village of Gulval (TR20 8YL). The garden is steep in places and not suitable for prams or wheelchairs. Wear good shoes and be prepared to walk. www.tremenheere.co.uk

TYNEHAM

Tyneham in Dorset is a curious place. It was once a bustling village with a post office, church and school. Today it's a ghost village, not quite there and not quite lost.

In 1943, the War Office commandeered the land around Tyneham for firing practice and all 225 residents were told to leave. They fully expected to return, but never did. In 1952 the War Office took out a compulsory purchase order on the area. From that day on Tyneham was frozen – the buildings began to crumble and the only inhabitants were the local wildlife.

Shocked villagers campaigned to return to their homes, but they weren't even allowed to visit. What was now the Ministry of Defence Lulworth Ranges remained closed until the 1970s. After years of campaigning, access to the village was finally reinstated for a few days each year, and a restoration effort focused on returning some life to Tyneham.

Now, the village has been made safe and is a popular spot for visitors and walkers. The rare white K1 phone box, designed by Sir George Gilbert Scott in 1921, is the first sign that this is not the modern world. Step inside the roofless cottages behind it and information boards explain that this used to be 'Post Office Row'. Stories from former

residents really bring the past to life, with archive photos of the village when it was thriving.

The school and church have been beautifully restored and are the only buildings now intact. In the school, where all ages were taught together, a 1920s schoolroom has been carefully recreated, with beautiful handwriting, uncomfortable desks and all. St Mary's Church across the way is similarly well-preserved, with lovely stained glass and a peaceful churchyard.

The ever-present stories of residents who lost their homes to help the war effort is a poignant reminder of sacrifices made. But on the other hand,

149

something unique has been preserved here, with Tyneham not having been modernised in any way – there are no cars or lampposts or satellite dishes. There aren't even litter bins and there is definitely no phone signal. But there is beauty and wildlife, and a taste of the past that can't be found anywhere else.

ACCESS AND OPENING TIMES

Tyneham is open to visitors on most weekends and public holidays. There is a car park and toilets at Tyneham Farm, but no other facilities. To get there, take the A352 from Dorchester/Wool or the A351 from Swanage/Corfe Castle. Follow signs towards Lulworth and look out for the steep turn to Tyneham. MoD road signs show if the ranges are open or closed. There's no postcode. www.tynehamopc.org.uk

The pub where time was never called

THE VALIANT SOLDIER

For more than 200 years, the Valiant Soldier in Buckfastleigh was a very normal pub. Pints were pulled, cigarettes were smoked and darts were thrown, same as countless public houses up and down the land.

Everything changed in 1965 when the brewery decided to close it. Mr Roberts, who had been the landlord for 30 years, called last orders for one last time and retreated upstairs to what was his family home.

After that, nothing changed. The Valiant Soldier was left completely untouched. Games of dominoes sat half-played, pint glasses went unwashed, and the optics waited to dispense their

next measure. What was once a thriving pub became a time capsule while the modern world moved on around it.

The fact that the Valiant Soldier was preserved like this is a modern miracle. When the building became available in 1997, Teignbridge District Council bought it for the local community.

A visit today shows an altogether simpler way of life. In the Public Bar there is a limited choice of beers and spirits for the men. The only pub food is peanuts, pies and pasties. Commodious ashtrays line the bar. For entertainment, cards and dominoes take the place of flat screen TVs and quiz machines. Across the hall, the lounge or 'snug' is more refined

with its Lloyd Loom chairs and linoleum floor, just waiting for some local ladies to come in for their Babychams.

Upstairs, the living quarters are similarly well preserved. Alice Roberts stayed here until the mid-1990s, living her daily life as she had always done. The kitchen boasts a gas-powered freezer and well stocked china cupboard. The cosy living room has no TV – a piano and wireless are quite enough for evenings spent sewing and writing letters. Mrs Roberts' wardrobe is a costume museum all of its own, and

the bathroom cabinet with its strange lotions and potions is an unexpectedly evocative insight into how things have changed in the last 50 years.

There is something very personal about the whole place, as if the residents have just stepped out of the room. The tiny details of their every day life paint the sort of picture that words could never do. Knowing this was someone's home makes imaginary conversations hang heavily in the air. It is only missing the breath of life.

Buckfastleigh Museum which adjoins

the Valiant Soldier, commemorates other aspects of local life from mining to the woollen industry and the Second World War. With support from English Heritage, volunteers and various grants and trusts, the building is once again a focus for the local community.

ACCESS AND OPENING TIMES

The Valiant Soldier is located at 80 Fore Street, Buckfastleigh, Devon TQ11 0BS. It is open daily from Easter to the end of October.

www.valiantsoldier.org.uk

WESTON-SUPER-MARE SAND SCULPTURES

Weston-super-Mare has become known as the sand sculpture capital of the UK. Its generous beaches and the sharp grain of its sand (not too sharp, they point out) make it perfect for sculpting as the grains lock together particularly well.

Started in 2005, the Sand Sculpture Festival has returned to Weston-super-Mare each year with sculptures on a theme such as Under the Sea, Story Time, and Fun N Games. For those keen to get their hands on sand, there are photo opportunities throughout the exhibition where you can join in with the sculptures.

If you're wondering how it's done, the exhibition will answer your questions with clear explanations of the building

technique and the feats of nature and engineering that help to create this fantastic display. It's true – only sand and water are used. The wires that you see are there to repel birds. And yes, they are strong enough to withstand the rain, and can easily last through a British summer.

Each sculpture takes roughly nine days to build, working eight hours a day. It doesn't half put your average sandcastle to shame. The creators are an international bunch of dedicated artists, some of whom also work in other mediums – from wood to ice and snow. Their sculptures are in demand worldwide, so Weston-super-Mare hosts quite the art show. A play area for schools lets everyone have a go at becoming a sand artist.

The display uses around 5000 tonnes of sand and the sculptures are bulldozed after the festival, so catch them while you can.

ACCESS AND OPENING TIMES

The Sand Sculpture Festival is located on the Marine Parade seafront in Weston-super-Mare (BS23 1BE) and runs from mid-April to the end of September. www.westonsandsculpture.co.uk

WORLD OF MODEL RAILWAYS

World of Model Railways in Mevagissey is a must for trainspotters of all ages. The extensive 00 gauge (1:76 scale) model railway display has more than 30 trains running through various different scenes. As befits its scale, it is a small space, densely-packed with detail, so allow enough time to appreciate it all.

There are trains of all shapes and sizes – electric and steam, old and new. Alongside the working miniature railways there are displays of modern trains from around the world, from sleek Japanese Shinkansen to functional Eastern European and classic London Underground models.

It's not just trains, oh no. The tracks are surrounded by model scenes of modern life, complete with traffic jams and breakdowns, kids going to school, commuters at stations, folks enjoying a sunny holiday, and even the Tour de France. All human life is here. There are idyllic scenes and functional moments – even model villagers need to go to the supermarket or drop off their recycling.

There are famous faces here too – look out for picnicking Sylvanian Families and

Thomas the Tank Engine and Friends in the Children's Railway. Many displays have buttons that allow visitors to liven up the scenes further.

There is all the fun of the fair here too with a spectacular miniature fairground complete with working Ferris Wheel. And don't miss the Ferrero Rocher Box diorama display. An annual competition is a challenge for miniature modellers to see who can create the most evocative scene in a small, clear rectangular chocolate box. The results are worthy of the ambassador's reception!

If the displays whet your appetite for creating your own model world there is a well-stocked shop on site with everything you need to get started. Run by real enthusiasts, World of Railways is fun for all the family.

ACCESS AND OPENING TIMES

World of Model Railways is on Meadow Street, Mevagissey, Cornwall PL26 6UL, not far from the harbour (parking available at Mevagissey's main car park). Open daily from the end of March to 1 October and on weekends through the winter.
www.model-railway.co.uk